THE LIBRARY OF
CONTEMPORARY
CHRISTIAN
MUSIC

EDITOR: WAYNE YANKIE

ORDER NO. SB1024
INTERNATIONAL STANDARD BOOK NUMBER: 978.1.59235.167.1

EXCLUSIVE DISTRIBUTORS:
MUSIC SALES CORPORATION
257 PARK AVENUE SOUTH, NEW YORK, NY 10010 USA
MUSIC SALES PTY., LIMITED
120 ROTHSCHILD STREET, ROSEBERY, SYDNEY, NSW 2018, AUSTRALIA

PRINTED IN THE UNITED STATES OF AMERICA BY
VICKS LITHOGRAPH AND PRINTING CORPORATION.

SHAWNEE PRESS
A PART OF THE MUSIC SALES GROUP
NEW YORK/LONDON/PARIS/SYDNEY/COPENHAGEN/BERLIN/TOKYO/MADRID

Contents

Dare You to Move

Words and Music by
JONATHAN FOREMAN

3rd (Last) time to Coda

How Great Is Our God

Words and Music by
CHRIS TOMLIN, JESSE REEVES and ED CASH

Big House

Words and Music b
MARK STUART, BARRY BLAIR
BOB HERMAN AND WILL McGINNIS

I don't know if you got a yard___ with a ham-mock in the shade.

2. I don't know if you got some shel - ter, say, a place___ to hide.
3. All I know, it's a big ol' house___ with rooms for ev - 'ry - one.

I don't know if you live with friends___ in whom you can___ con - fide.
All I know, is___ lots of land,___ where we can play___ and run.

Holy Is the Lord

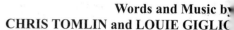

Words and Music by
CHRIS TOMLIN and LOUIE GIGLIO

I Can Only Imagine

Words and Music by
BART MILLARD

He Reigns

Words and Music
PETER FURLE
and STEVE TAYLC

D.S. al Coda

Mary, Did You Know?

Words by MARK LOWRY

Music by BUDDY GREENE

I Believe

Words and Music
NATALIE GRA

38

Jesus Freak

Words and Music
TOBY McKEEHA
and MARK HEIMERMA

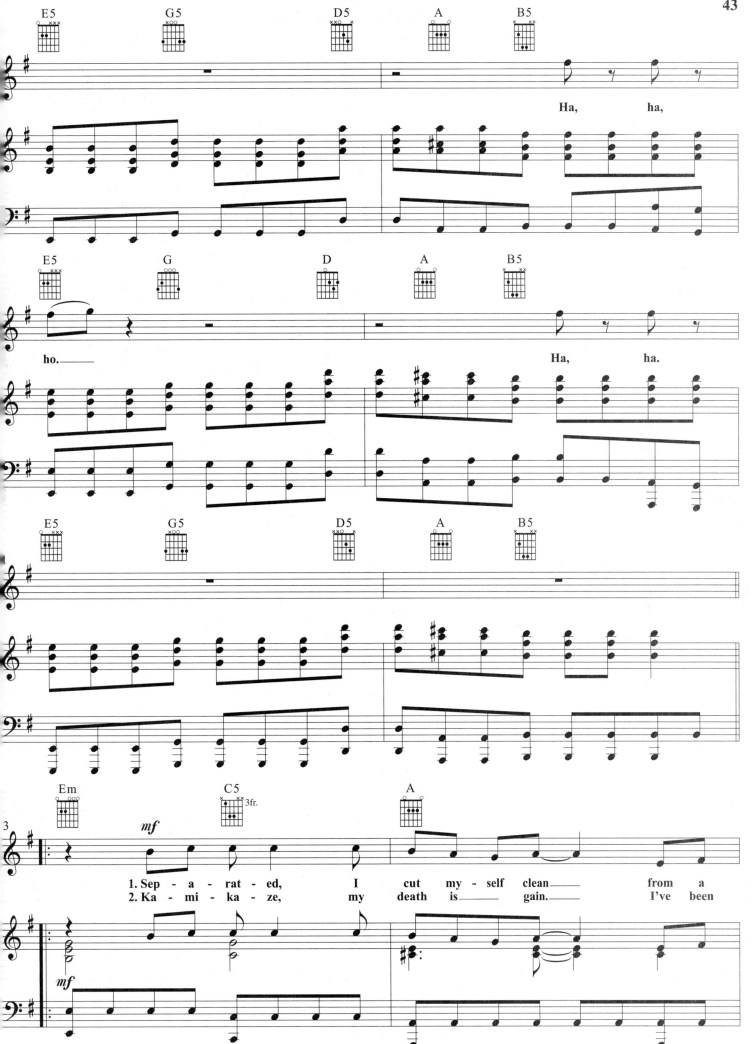

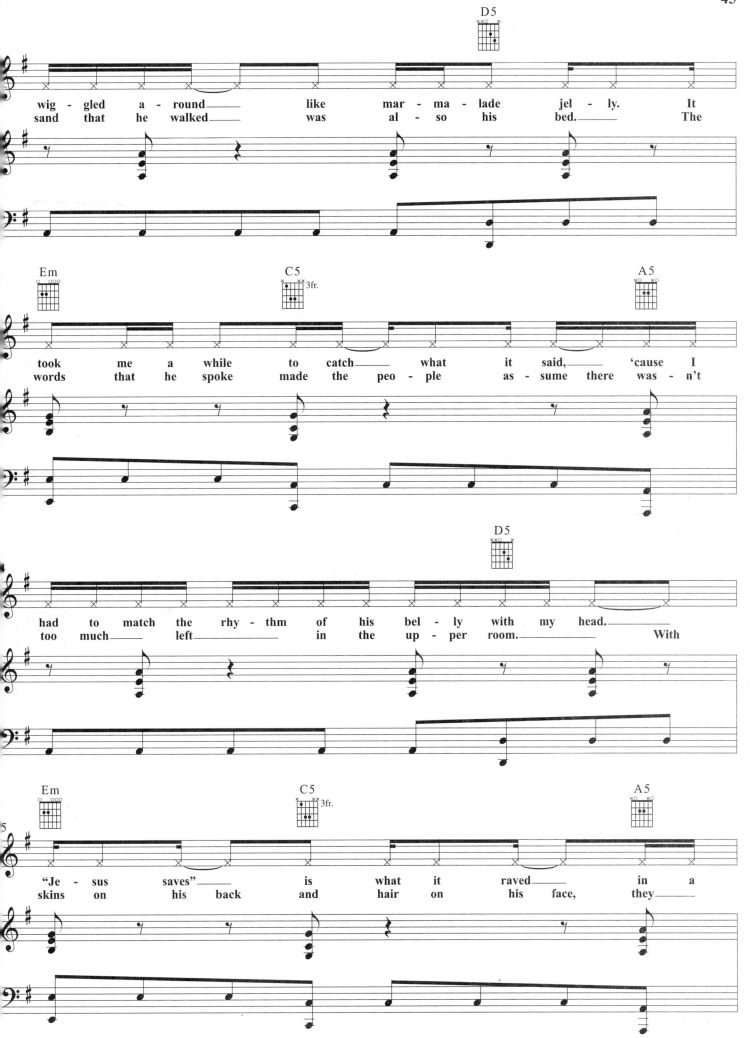

45

26

D5

typ - i - cal tat - too green. He____
thought he was strange____ by the lo - custs he ate. You see, the

27

Em   C5   A5

stood on a box in the mid - dle of the cit - y and he
phar - i - sees tripped when they heard him____ speak,____ un - til the

28

claimed he had____ a dream.____
king took the head of this Je - sus freak.

29 *f*

E5   G5   D5   A5   B5

What will peo - ple think____ when they hear that I'm____ a Je - sus freak?

f

my best Friend was born___ in a man - ger? ___ in a man - ger?___

D.S. al Coda

CODA

What will peo - ple think?___

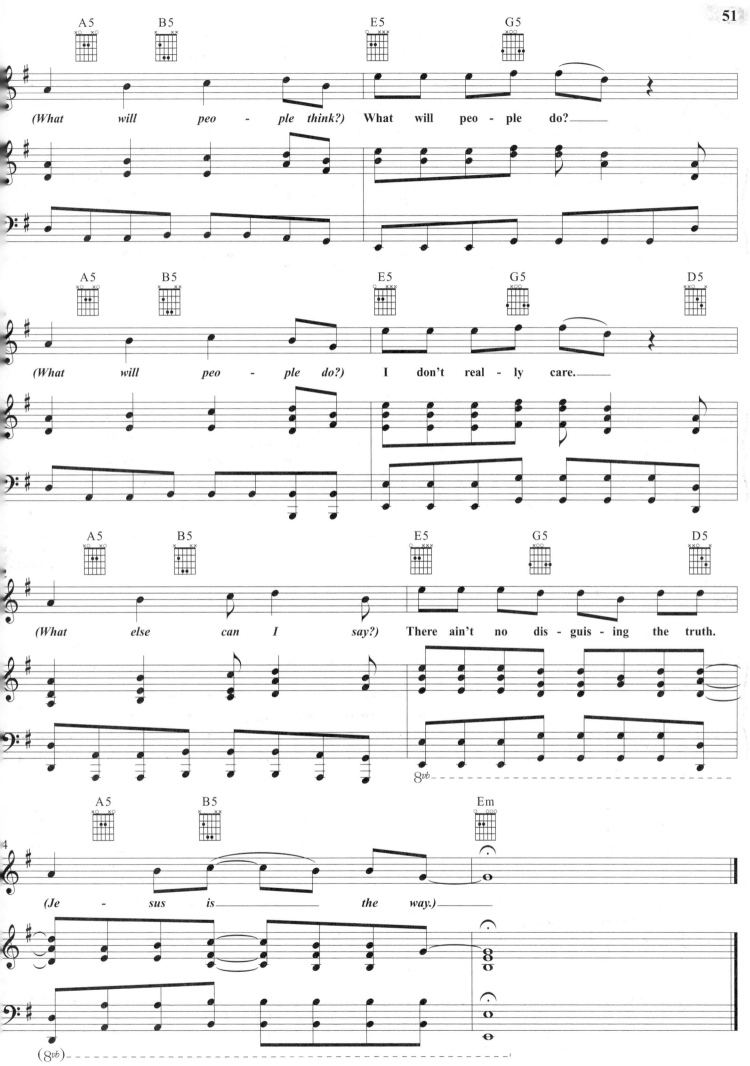

Held

Words and Music
CHRISTA WELI

One Child

Gently, with much emotion ♩ = 104

Words and Music by
DAVID MULLEN *and* **MICHAEL HUNTER OCHS**

Beautiful One

Words and Music
TIM HUGH...

Indescribable

Words and Music by LAURA STO...
Additional Lyrics by JESSE REEV...

Butterfly Kisses

Words and Music
BOB CARLISLE and RANDY THOMA

80

Gsus$^4_2$ G   Gsus$^4_2$ G

1. 2. but - ter - fly___ kiss - es   af - ter bed - time   pray'r.___   Stick - in'
3. but - ter - fly___ kiss - es   with her mom - ma   there,___

Gsus$^4_2$ G   D/G   Esus$^4_2$ Em   D

lit - tle white___ flow - ers all   up in her   hair.
2. "You

C   G2/B   G/B

1. "Walk be - side___ the po - ny, Dad - dy. It's my___ first ride.   I
(2.) know how much___ I love___ you, Dad - dy, but if you don't mind,___ I'm
3. "Walk me down___ the aisle,___ Dad - dy. It's just a - bout time.   Does my

C   G2/B   G/B   G/D

know the cake___ looks fun - ny, Dad - dy, but I___ sure tried."___   Oh, with
on - ly gon - na kiss___ you on___ the cheek___ this time."___
wed - ding gown___ look pret - ty, Dad - dy?___ Dad - dy, don't cry."___

82

Come, Now Is the Time to Worship

Words and Music by
BRIAN DOERKSEN

85

Awaken

Words and Music
NATALIE GRANT, ROB GRAVE
JASON McARTHUR *and* **JOY WILLIAM**

Better Is One Day

Words and Music b
MATT REDMA

Forever

Words and Music b
CHRIS TOMLI

G
Am/G G Am/G
G
car - ry on. His love en - dures for - ev - er. Sing
D/F♯
C2/E
42
praise, sing praise. Sing
D(no3)
C2(no3)
D.S. al Coda
f
46
praise, sing praise. For - ev -
CODA
G(no3)
50
- er.

Dive

Words and Music by
STEVEN CURTIS CHAPMAN

Driving, with energy ♩ = 90 - 100

1. The long a - wait - ed rains___ have

fall - en hard___ up - on___ the thirst - y ground;___ they've carved their way to where___ the wild___

Above All

Words and Music by
PAUL BALOCHE and **LENNY LeBLANC**

All About You

Words and Music
ISRAEL HOUGHTON and CINDY CRUSE-RATCLIFF

114

God of Wonders

Words and Music by
MARC BYRD and STEVE HINDALONG

Holy, Holy, Holy

Faith

Words and Music b
REUBEN MORGA

Lamb of God

Words and Music by
TWILA PARI

Be the Centre

Words and Music
MICHAEL FRY

I Could Sing of Your Love Forever

Words and Music by
MARTIN SMITH

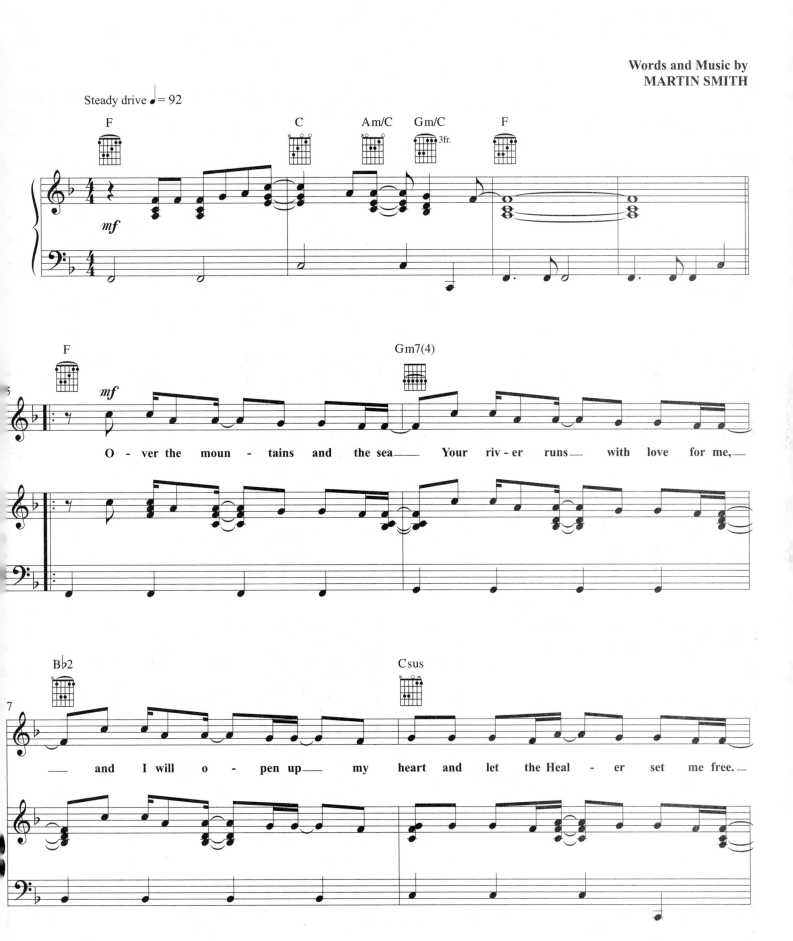

Captured

Words and Music
BERNIE HERMS, JASON McARTHUR *and* ROB GRAVE

With a driving beat (♩ = 88)

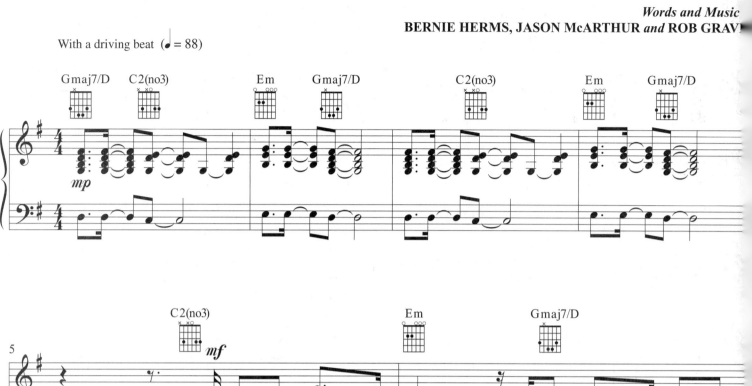

It must mean some - thing;___ when I close my___ eyes

___ vi - sions of ___ You come ___ to me and flood ___ my mind.___

It must mean some - thing;___ when my heart is___ true,___

all that I___ can think___ a - bout___ is You.___

Ev - 'ry - where I go,___ You find___ me. E - ven when I run,___ I'm cap -

Hungry
(Falling on My Knees)

Words and Music
KATHRYN SCOT

With a groove ♩ = 86 - 90

1. Hun - gry, I come to You, for I know You sat - is - fy.
2. Bro - ken, I run to You, for Your arms are o - pen wide;

I am emp - ty, but I know Your love
I am wear - y, but I know Your touch

The Heart of Worship

Words and Music by
MATT REDMAN

Did You Feel the Mountains Tremble?

Words and Music by
MARTIN SMITH

Fling wide, you heav-en-ly gates; pre-pare the

way of the ris-en Lord.

O - pen up the doors and let the mu-

-sic play. Let the streets re - sound with

Place in This World

Words and Music by
ANY GRANT, WAYNE KIRKPATRICK
and MICHAEL W. SMITH

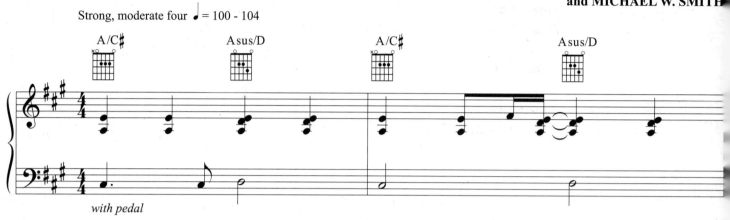

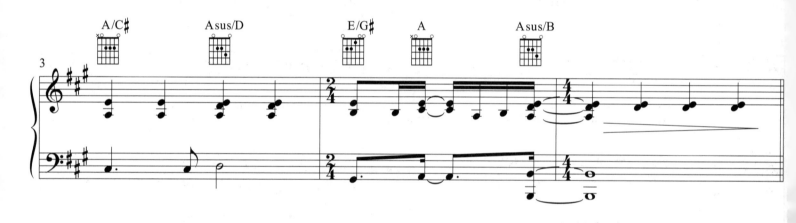

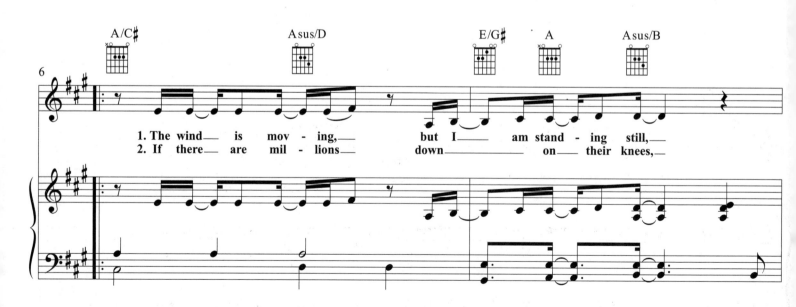

1. The wind is mov-ing, but I am stand-ing still,
2. If there are mil-lions down on their knees,

He Is Exalted

Words and Music b
TWILA PARI

We Want to See Jesus Lifted High

**Words and Music by
DOUG HORLEY**

You Are My King

(Amazing Love)

Words and Music by
BILLY JAMES FOOT

In Christ Alone

**Words and Music by
STUART TOWNEND and KEITH GETTY**

Something Beautiful

Words and Music
MATTHEW WES
and CHANCE SCOGGIN

Here I Am to Worship

Words and Music
TIM HUGHE

You're Worthy of My Praise

Words and Music by
DAVID RUIS

Lord, Reign in Me

Words and Music by
BRENTON BROWN

1. O - ver all the earth You reign on high,
2. O - ver ev - 'ry thought, o - ver ev - 'ry word,

ev - 'ry moun - tain stream, ev - 'ry sun - set sky.
may my life re - flect the beau - ty of my Lord.

Draw Me Close

Easy two feel ♩ = 72-76

Words and Music by
KELLY CARPENTER

to hear You say___ that I'm___ Your friend.___
to feel the warmth___ of Your___ em - brace.___

Help me find___ the way;___ bring me back___ to You.

Awesome God

Words and Music by
RICHARD MULLINS

Alive

Words and Music b
MATT BRONLEEW
and REBECCA St. JAME

196

Hallelujah
(Your Love Is Amazing)

Words and Music by
BRENTON BROWN and BRIAN DOERKSEN

Breathe

Words and Music by
MARIE BARNETT

Lord, I Lift Your Name on High

Words and Music b
RICK FOUND

We Fall Down

Words and Music b[y]
CHRIS TOMLI[N]

Flood

Words and Music
CHARLIE LOWELL, DAN HASELTINE
MATT ODMARK, and STEPHEN MASON

los - ing con - trol.____ Dark sky all a - round;____

D.S. al Coda 𝄋

can't feel my feet touch - ing the ground.____ But if

CODA A6 NC

- ing a - gain.____

You Are My All in All

Words and Music by
DENNIS JERNIGAN

Stomp

Lifesong

228

Oh Lord, You're Beautiful

Words and Music by
KEITH GREEN

Thank You

Words and Music by
RAY BOLTZ